Theorising Quality in Higher Education

The Bedford Way Papers Series

1 *Music Education: Trends and issues*
  Edited by Charles Plummeridge
2 *Perspectives on School Effectiveness and School Improvement*
  Edited by John White and Michael Barber
3 *Education, Environment and Economy: Reporting research in a new academic grouping*
  Edited by Frances Slater, David Lambert and David Lines
4 *Exploring Futures in Initial Teacher Education: Changing key for changing times*
  Edited by Andy Hudson and David Lambert
5 *50 Years of Philosophy of Education: Progress and prospects*
  Edited by Graham Haydon
6 *Men as Workers in Services for Young Children: Issues of a mixed gender workforce*
  Edited by Charlie Owen, Claire Cameron and Peter Moss
7 *Convergence and Divergence in European Education and Training Systems*
  Andy Green, Alison Wolf and Tom Leney
8 *FE and Lifelong Learning: Realigning the sector for the twenty-first century*
  Edited by Andy Green and Norman Lucas
9 *Values and Educational Research*
  Edited by David Scott
10 *The Culture of Change: Case studies of improving schools in Singapore and London*
   Peter Mortimore, Saravanan Gopinathan, Elizabeth Leo, Kate Myers, Leslie Sharpe, Louise Stoll and Jo Mortimore
11 *Education and Employment: The DfEE and its place in history*
   Edited by Richard Aldrich, David Crook and David Watson
12 *The Maths We Need Now: Demands, deficits and remedies*
   Edited by Clare Tikly and Alison Wolf
13 *Why Learn Maths?*
   Edited by Steve Bramall and John White
14 *History of Education for the Twenty-First Century*
   Edited by David Crooks and Richard Aldrich
15 *The Children of London: Attendance and welfare at school 1870–1990*
   Susan Williams, Patrick Ivin and Caroline Morse
16 *Developing Inclusive Schooling: Perspectives, policies and practice*
   Edited by Carol Campbell
17 *School Textbook Research: The case of geography 1800–2000*
   Norman Graves
18 *Changing Britain, Changing Lives: Three generations at the turn of the century*
   Edited by Elsa Ferri, John Bynner and Michael Wadsworth
19 *Teacher Pay and Performance*
   Peter Dolton, Steve McIntosh and Arnaud Chevalier
20 *Childhood in Generational Perspective*
   Edited by Berry Mayall and Hela Zeihar
21 *Homework: The evidence*
   Susan Hallam
22 *Teaching in Further Education: New perspectives for a changing context*
   Norman Lucas
23 *Legalised Leadership: Law-based educational reform in England and its effect on headteachers*
   Dan Gibton
24 *Theorising Quality in Higher Education*
   Louise Morley

Theorising Quality in Higher Education

Louise Morley

Bedford Way Papers

INSTITUTE OF
EDUCATION
UNIVERSITY OF LONDON

First published in 2004 by the Institute of Education, University of London,
20 Bedford Way, London WC1H 0AL
www.ioe.ac.uk/publications

© Institute of Education, University of London 2004

Over 100 years of excellence in education

British Library Cataloguing in Publication Data:
A catalogue record for this publication is available from the British Library

ISBN 0 85473 706 5

Louise Morley asserts the moral right to be identified as the author of this work.

All rights reserved. No part of this publication may be reproduced, stored in a retrieval system, or transmitted in any form or by any means, electronic, mechanical, photocopying, recording or otherwise, without the prior permission of the copyright owner.

Text design by Joan Rose
Cover design by Andrew Chapman
Page make-up by Cambridge Photosetting Services, Cambridge

Production services by
Book Production Consultants plc, Cambridge

Printed by Piggott Black Bear Ltd.

Contents

Acknowledgements		vi
List of abbreviations		vii
1	**The political economy of higher education**	1
	Quality as policy technology	1
	The global market	5
2	**How did this happen?**	8
	Managing risk and manufacturing panic	8
	Continuous improvement: adding value or self-beratement	10
	Consuming by numbers	12
3	**Getting it right**	14
	The genesis of the quality assurance movement	14
	Thoroughly modern methods?	19
4	**Reining in**	21
	Accountability, autonomy and the audit culture	21
	Regulating research	23
	Performance indicators: the myth of measurement	26
5	**The political is personal**	30
	The psychic economy of quality	30
	Performativity and the power of discourse	32
	The stress of split focusing	36
6	**In the long term**	38
References		41

Acknowledgements

Thanks to my colleagues in the Centre for Higher Education Studies and to those in the School for Educational Foundations and Policy Studies for their support and encouragement to produce critical texts on quality in higher education. Thanks to my doctoral students and the students on the MA in Higher and Professional Education for all the stimulating discussions on quality in the academy. Thanks to my network of feminist academics including Miriam David, Rosemary Deem, Debbie Epstein, Diana Leonard, Mairead Dunne, Meg Maguire and Naz Rassool for their intellectual and personal support. Thanks to Simeon Underwood for sending me his extensive personal archive of newspaper articles on quality assurance. Thanks to Deborah Spring and her colleagues in the Institute of Education Publications Office for their helpful editorial feedback.

Abbreviations

AUT	Association of University Teachers
CNAA	Council for National Academic Awards
CVCP	Committee of Vice Chancellors and Principals
DES	Department of Education and Science
DfES	Department for Education and Skills
DfEE	Department for Education and Employment
EC	European Commission
HEFCE	Higher Education Funding Council for England
HEQC	Higher Education Quality Council
ILT	Institute of Learning and Teaching
OECD	Organisation for Economic Co-operation and Development
QAA	Quality Assurance Agency
RAE	Research Assessment Exercise
TQA	Teaching Quality Assessment
TQM	Total Quality Management
UFC	Universities Funding Council
UGC	University Grants Committee
UNESCO	United Nations Education, Science and Cultural Organisation

1 The political economy of higher education

Quality as policy technology

The political economy of higher education is changing. Higher education has been restructured and reformed to meet the perceived requirements of a globalised knowledge economy. Changes in the political economy have forced radical structural readjustment in the public services since the early 1980s in Britain, with a move towards privatisation, contract government, output-based funding and the marketisation of services. The surface rationality used to justify the need for more structured systems of management in higher education is the increased size and complexity of the global higher education system. Elitist interpretations imply that quality was assured in the past by restricting admission practices. Now, new constituencies, consumers, partnerships and rainbow coalitions of stakeholders threaten to make the whole system unwieldy. Hence an increasing emphasis on management processes in higher education and the functional management of intellectual labour (Dominelli and Hoogvelt 1996). Part of neo-liberal reform has involved the alignment of public sector organisations with the values, structures and management processes of the private sector.

Economics, rather than sociology, is the dominant disciplinary influence on higher education policy in Britain. Budget maximisation, rather than social justice and social transformation, are guiding principles. The emphasis on value-added or best value approach means that questions are posed about whether institutions are delivering the best educational value possible given their resources and student intake, and whether they are continuously improving their provision and meeting goals and targets. Traditionally, higher education institutions have enjoyed a fairly high degree of self-regulation. However, self-regulation has been seen more and more as representing the private interests of the sector, rather than public interests. The state has moved from being a provider of public services to a regulator or auditor of them. Quality assurance agencies in different national locations are now charged with the responsibility of protecting both state and consumer interests. They attempt to ensure that government funds are well spent and that contractual obligations with students and with the state are met.

In the changing political economy of higher education, the educational good is being standardised and represented as a knowable commodity that can be exchanged in the global market. Reputation is a market variable and is increasingly being constructed via quality scores. Furthermore, the educational good is now ostensibly available to a more diverse global population across national and social boundaries. Regulation and standardisation are positioned as antidotes to the potential chaos and risk of the mass higher education and commercialisation of the sector. A central mechanism for standardisation is quality assurance.

Quality combines with funding arrangements to become a powerful metanarrative. Quality parades as a cultural logic and universal truth and therefore continually extends its domain. As part of neoliberal reform of the public services, it is spreading across the globe like a policy epidemic (Levin 1998). Quality assurance links the micro world of the organisation with the public world of policy and politics. It is an installation of power, with monolithic notions of what constitutes quality.

Disguising how power works is one of the key features of what Foucault called 'political technology' (Dreyfus and Rabinow 1982), which is when structures and systems are put in place to facilitate political ideologies, for example new managerialism. Quality procedures translate particular rationalities and moralities into new forms of governance and professional behaviour. As such, quality is a political technology functioning as a regime and relay of power – that is, it serves as both a mechanism and ideology through which certain values, behaviours and structures are prescribed. Political technologies, with their norms and common-sense assumptions, disguise how power works. Ball (2003) argues that there are three interrelated policy technologies underpinning educational reform: the market, managerialism and performativity. I argue that quality assurance is where all three policy technologies converge.

Policy technologies create norms. Norms can constitute an invisible web of power because the norms become internalised and more difficult to recognise and contest (Shore and Wright 1999). An example of a norm is that it is now widely accepted that a major signifier of academic excellence and indeed productivity is a good publication record in certain academic journals. Individuals and organisations have learned to self-monitor and maximise themselves. They manage risk, productivity and performance in accordance with the changing cultural logic of the sector. The psychic operation of the norm can offer a more insidious route for regulatory power than explicit coercion (Butler 1997). The quality project involves correction, rehabilitation and cognitive restructuring. It evokes a common language of aspiration. Ball (2003) argues that deregulation is really re-regulation. While it appears that the market rather than the state is the dominant force in the public services, this actually requires organisations and individuals to conform and demonstrate their value to market consumers within prescribed performance indicators. In terms of quality assurance, there is massive over-regulation. There is a pincer movement throughout the public services, with professionals caught between a 'poisonous combination of under-resourcing and over-regulation' (Cameron 2003: 133).

There has been a re-formation of the academic *habitus* itself. The OECD (1995: 74) called for a 'devolved environment' which 'requires a shift by central management bodies toward setting the overall framework rather than micromanaging ... and changes in attitudes and behaviour on both sides'. Gale and Kitto (2003) argue that the imperative for a market disposition has devalued the cultural capital of academics and that pure critique is no longer sufficient as an academic product. Preoccupation with quality is one aspect of the market disposition. Quality in the academy, with its monitoring systems, quantitative scores, production of information, and performance management has involved significant rehabilitation of the labour force. Audit, by evaluating performance and effectiveness makes judgements about organisations' and individuals' value and worth.

Who controls the judgements is an issue of power. The process, while appearing rational and technocratic, carries the possibility of considerable misrecognition, unfairness and humiliation.

There is a psychic economy of quality assurance. (Psychic economy means that emotions and emotional commitment need to be activated and invested in the process, for example guilt, pride, shame, etc.) The discourse has cognitive authority and considerable emotional power (Howie 2002). Existing professional practices are rendered fragile or untrustworthy. Professionals are valued for their contribution to organisational performance within set frameworks, rather than for their knowledge base or affective skills. Hence there is a new moral economy. Quality procedures require the activation and exploitation of a range of feelings such as guilt, loyalty, desire, greed, shame, anxiety and responsibilisation, in the service of effectiveness and point-scoring (Ozga and Walker 1999). There are profound ontological issues at stake in the scoring of organisations. The translation of higher educational activities into cash terms and league tables with exchange value establishes new relations of power (Bowden 2000). Pedagogical, social and interpersonal relations are changing as a consequence of the introduction of the customer care revolution, new competitions between individuals and organisations for research funding and student numbers. In line with post-Fordist employment regimes, the two accounting systems in the UK (research productivity and teaching and learning) can lead to split focusing for academics, who have to be increasingly multiskilled. Work intensification combines with complex value systems to produce a silencing of opposition. Indeed, opposition itself is a devalued capital in the market economy. The association of quality assurance with highly desirable procedures such as transparency and accountability disguises the power relations and plays down the coercive and punitive implications. Transparency implies a challenge to the discriminatory practices of the hidden curriculum (Margolis 2001). Yet it also implies a truth to be un/dis covered and conceals the way in which texts are socially constructed and are therefore read and interpreted in multiple ways. While transparency and accountability have become 'hooray' words, the accountability can often be a one-way gaze, with a marked lack of accountability of assessors and agencies regulating quality assurance.

The positive connotations of the word 'quality' makes it hard to resist. Like other neoliberal discourses, e.g. choice and consumer empowerment, quality assurance appears to be client-focused and democratising, whereas it has deeply conservative underpinnings. Quality assurance is constructed as part of the modernisation process. As such, critics can be accused of golden-ageism. However, only certain aspects of the academy are being detraditionalised, with gender inequalities remaining firmly intact on a fairly global basis, for example (Morley 2004). Yet resistance to neoliberal change is perceived as an incapacity for readjustment and redeployment in a rapidly changing social and economic world. There is a powerful rhetoric of inevitability and macrodeterminism in quality assurance procedures, or a TINA effect (There Is No Alternative) (Bauman 2001b). The apparent commonsense logic means that resistance is hard to mobilise. Terms that are used to describe organisational life in the academy are also active forces shaping it. There is an idealisation embedded in quality assurance. Yet the culture of excellence, with its required compliance and performativity, could be resulting in mediocrity.

The global market

Quality assessment is positioned as the antithesis to the chaos of global expansion and mobility in higher education. The various information flows of globalisation also mean that opportunities for policy borrowing and convergence have been greatly enhanced. Lingard (2000) points out how international organisations, including the OECD and the World Bank, function as instruments of policy as they act as institutionalising mechanisms for the new global educational policy consensus. There are particular policy networks and traffic flows across national boundaries, e.g. the European Union, Commonwealth countries, and Anglophone regions. International agencies serve to globalise neoliberalism. The World Bank's report on higher education (1994) suggested that countries should shift from one source of funding for higher education, and should attempt to raise funds from student fees, endowments, and consultancies. The report stated that higher education globally should resemble the United States model more closely.

Universities have become more prominent in their contribution to the globalised knowledge economy. Globalisation impacts on higher education and *vice versa*. Deem (2001) argues that changes in funding regimes, organisational and cultural changes, new forms of educational provision through the Internet or the inclusion of new groups of students are the central effects of globalisation on higher education. Democratising policies on inclusiveness alongside economic imperatives for upskilling mean that universally there is a move to widen access and participation in higher education (UNESCO 1998). There is also a growing mobility of students. UNESCO (1998) estimates that 1.6 million people were enrolled in higher education outside their own countries at the end of the 1990s. Global consumers are thought to require condensed and reliable information about the product that they are purchasing. Enhanced student mobility via national and international credit transfer agreements such as the Bologna Declaration (1999) means that qualifications have to be more knowable and, indeed, transferable.

Change in higher education is also being driven by the needs of large transnational companies and related knowledge-based industries. Polster (2000: 19) calls this the 'corporatization agenda'. Boundaries between the academy, government and business have been loosened and reformulated in what is sometimes known as the 'triple helix' (Etzkowitz and Leydesdorff 1997). Corporate interests play a more powerful role in determining the purposes of higher education. While higher education in Britain is still largely dependent on state funding, it is expected to meet the requirements of the private sector economy. There are multiple linkages between the different stakeholders in the economy, and universities are being increasingly encouraged to work with industry and commerce to generate knowledge, wealth and regional and national economies (Coaldrake 2000; Coate *et al.* 2000). Today, boundaries between disciplines and professional knowledges are continuing to shift. Professional knowledge has become unstable. This notion is not entirely new. Lyotard

(1984) argued that all knowledge is narrative because it changes so rapidly. The changing political economy combined with changing demands from employers means that higher education is becoming an ever-increasingly risky business.

2 How did this happen?

Managing risk and manufacturing panic

Higher education in societies in transition, such as South Africa, is represented in terms of transformation and renewal (Cooper and Subotsky 2001). However, in the West, there is often a discourse of crisis, loss, damage, contamination and decay in higher education. There are images of the university in ruins (Readings 1996), the 'degradation' of academia (Nisbet 1971), the university 'in crisis' (Sommer 1995), higher education 'at risk' (Manicas 1998); the death of autonomy (Dill 2001) and proletarianisation (Dearlove 1997). Massification, industrialisation and the more overt linkage of higher education with the needs of commerce and industry are seen as having polluted the purity of elite organisations of knowledge production. The university is now one provider in a learning market. Universities have to open their doors to new constituencies, new competitions and new risks. One of the emerging functions of higher education has become the aversion of risk.

The academy, like other public services, has become a site of social anxiety and fear. Institutions no longer connote safety. The construct of trustworthiness is being associated with standardisation, competence, continuity and reliability. Professional contexts today are characterised as low trust/high risk cultures. The risk society has resulted in the decline of trust in professional conduct. Quality assurance in industry aims for zero defect and error reduction and prevention. The same principle is being applied to the public services. Issues of trust, authority and expertise have been disaggregated. Routine, rather than deviant, practices have been subjected to scrutiny. Academics have lost some of their authoritative power. The advantage is that powerful groups are being held more to account. The disadvantage is that success criteria for complex public

How did this happen?

services are being reduced and manipulated into over-simplistic classifications and service-level agreements. A new defensiveness is emerging.

Quality assurance is a model of panic creation or a 'synthetic panic' (Jenkins, 1999: 8–9). The moral panic over standards was captured in a speech made by John Pattern when he was the Secretary of State for Education in 1994, to the Committee of Vice Chancellors and Principals (CVCP). He called on the Higher Education Quality Council (HEQC) to place more emphasis on broad compatibility in the standards offered by different institutions. In 1994 the HEQC set up a Graduate Standards Programme to develop threshold standards for degrees. A review was also commissioned, and in 1996 it reported that degree standards varied significantly between universities and even within one institution (HEQC 1997; Lucas and Webster, 1998). This was part of a wider move to regulate the public services as a whole.

It is questionable whether policy is a response to existing conditions and problems, or a discourse in which both problems and solutions are created (Bacchi 2000). Quality assurance is a response to the moral panic over standards, massification, wealth creation and globalisation. Heightened concern is a prerequisite for panic. There is political potential in crises and catastrophes. Politicians can demonstrate their effectiveness via quantitative measures of 'improvement' in the public services. With moral panic, authorities, including politicians and managers, either play a central role in initiating it, or are likely to join ongoing arrangements and derive some benefit from them, such as a more docile workforce. Beck explains:

> In an age of uncertainty, discourses that appear to promise a resolution to ambivalence by producing identifiable victims and blameable villains are likely to figure prominently in the State's ceaseless attempts to impose social order.
>
> (Beck 1997: 265)

McRobbie (1994: 199) identifies two main responses to panic. The first is the 'fortress mentality that is characterised by a feeling of helplessness, political powerlessness and paralysis'. The second is the 'gung-ho' approach, the 'something must be done about it' mindset. The latter could exemplify the quality mongers (Hart 1997). This is the group of people from which the pool of peer assessors, quality assurance officers and managers is drawn. This group can be driven by paradoxical and contradictory aims; they occupy multiple subject positions. On the one hand, they subscribe to processes that are profoundly undemocratic and authoritarian. On the other hand, there is a democratising driver. They want a better deal for students – more information, product specification and risk reduction in a knowledge-driven economy. The values of the consumer society are now firmly embedded in educational relationships (Baudrillard 1998).

Continuous improvement: adding value or self-beratement?

Consumer interests are seen to benefit from continuous improvement. The quality agenda and the culture of continuous improvement in public services have resulted in the need for professionals to evaluate and represent their practice and organisations within new modes of description. The debate on standards, accountability, customer care and transparency of decision-making in the professions is demanding enhanced skills relating to representation, measurement, resource management and evaluation. A culture of evidence-based practice and an economic climate of best value are emerging. Quality assurance and continuous improvement are powerful policy condensates, demanding consensus and orthodoxy. They exemplify the steering-at-a-distance trend in public policy whereby education is more overtly tied in to national economic interests, while giving the appearance of site-based and/or individual autonomy (Ball 1998).

The public services, initially in the USA, and later in Britain followed Deming's beliefs (1986), that his total quality approach was equally applicable to manufacturing and to services (Billing and Thomas 1998). However, higher education adopted management processes from the private sector long after they had been tried and abandoned by corporations (Birnbaum 2000). The early 1990s saw a proliferation of literature in the USA that berated total quality management (TQM) as too expensive, bureaucratic and unreliable (Brigham 1993; Harari 1993; Keller 1992).

Shore and Selwyn (1998: 165) believe that in academia, TQA (teaching quality assessment) has become 'practically homonymous with TQM'. However, the concept of improvement in quality assurance can often seem under-theorised in the context of sophisticated analyses in the academy of measurement techniques. For example, Strathern writes:

> 'Improvement' is wonderfully open-ended, for it at once describes efforts and results. And it invites one to make both ever more effective – a process from which the tests themselves are not immune: measuring the improvement leads to improving the measures.
>
> (Strathern 1997: 307)

Improvement is linked to commensurable increase. There is a question here about the endpoint in continuous improvement, with an underlying sense of the permanence of struggle, the elusiveness of satisfactory goals, and the ambiguity of measurement procedures.

Continuous improvement has a surface agenda that is credible and desirable in the context of global changes and the risk society. However, continuous improvement also has a subtextual agenda that could be theorised in terms of the Foucauldian concept of governmentability. It is an example of capillary power in that it is everywhere and permeates organisational priorities, social relations and personal and professional aspirations. The language and ethos of quality assurance often appears to have quasi-religious connotations, implying lack, deficit, rescue and renewal. This is reminiscent of the Christian notion of original sin. It takes a professional lifetime to a redeem oneself. Closure is infinitely deferred. There is interest in the utility value or 'just-in-time' rather than 'just-in-case' skills and competencies. Hence the rapid change agenda creates what Barnett (2000) describes as 'supercomplexity'. The sense of tumultuous urgency can create panic and feelings of inadequacy for those struggling to keep on top of changes. The individual is in perpetual motion, never allowed to stand still. Workers have to internalise the demand for flexibility.

An aspect of the modernisation of higher and professional education is the attempt to link the work and aspirations of individuals with the goals of the organisation. Barnett (2000) believes that knowledge is now less important for the professional than attitude and the disposition to respond to change. There is a complex relationship between the individual and the collective. Professionals are being encouraged to develop individual learning strategies and, increasingly, to practice the art of self-observation. Sennett (1998) argues that higher education is rapidly becoming the ally of a ruthless economic system in which individuals are expected to re- and upskill with no continuity of identity, security or purpose. Another argument is that higher education helps individuals to survive in changing settings. Whereas the locus of change appears to be the individual, the individual is now also more accountable to the collective via quality procedures and scores. Teaching quality and research productivity have been converted from individual professional responsibility to the collective interests of institutions and departments (Henkel 1999). Quality assurance, as part of new managerialism, involves the responsibilisation of every organisational member. The organisation, or unit of analysis, becomes the reflexive project for which all organisational members are responsible.

Consuming by numbers

The consumer paradigm is demanding much greater transparency in performance data than before. In the chaos of marketisation and massification, quality scores provide a point of identification. Complex information about quality is scored and organised into at-a-glance league tables that are widely published in the popular press (Berry 1999). Categoric ratings are converted into numerical variables. The stratification of institutions has become more visible and more precisely differentiated, and the consequences more tangible (Henkel 1999). Tomlin (1998: 204) argues that 'league tables hold a morbid fascination'. Scores and league tables travel the world and can sometimes inform decision-making and choice of organisations and courses. They contribute to reputation and international status. Students are constructed as rational economic agents – making choices about investments.

Scoring, it seems, can have both material and affective consequences that cohere to make the workforce more governable. There is a convergence between description and prescription as organisations strategise to achieve high scores. Scores represent symbolic and, in the case of the RAE, material capital. Their value is the extent to which they communicate and recognise shared meanings. The score is a form of gift exchange – a high score is a gift from outside. A low score is a counter-gift. The limited appeals procedures mean that scores are irreversible time capsules – imbued with authority and prescribed meaning. Scoring implies that quality is a quantifiable object and can be subjected to the rules of accountancy.

3 Getting it right

The genesis of the quality assurance movement

Quality assurance is not new. It was originally an integral part of craftspersonship and professionalism. More recently, it has been disaggregated from the professions, formalised and transformed into an object of inquiry (Hart 1997). In Britain, quality assessment exists 'to ensure that all education for which the Higher Education Funding Council provides funding is of satisfactory quality or better, and to ensure speedy rectification of unsatisfactory quality', the main aim being to 'inform funding and reward excellence' (HEFCE 1992, 1993).

Universities have possessed various forms of internal and external mechanisms for assuring the quality of their work. The external examiners' system has traditionally been a form of quality assurance. Silver (1993) researched peer assessment in higher education, and found that it was a fairly haphazard business, with no clear demonstration of common standards. While the external examiners' system could have been characterised in terms of Cameron and Ettington's (1988) concept of *adhocracy*, there is little evidence to demonstrate that the development of quality systems was in response to *serious* quality problems in the sector (Trow 1994).

A more cynical view is that quality assurance was introduced as a regulatory device for the process of production rather than as a check on the quality of the product itself. The education reform of the schools sector in Britain in the 1980s was soon followed by political concerns over the regulation of quality and standards in higher education. Kogan and Hanney (2000) argue that perhaps no area of public policy has been subjected to such radical changes over the last 20 years as higher education. In 1983 the Reynolds Committee was set up to consider academic standards in higher education. It reported in 1986 with formal codes of practice covering external examiners and postgraduate studies (Hodson and Thomas 1999). Between 1992 and 1994 14 influential reports about the future of higher education were published. The content of these reports addresses immediate requirements for change caused by a mass higher education system (HEFCE 1993), a changing student population (NIACE 1993) and longer-term requirements arising out of economic and social imperatives.

In 1991 the government's White Paper *Higher Education: A new framework* set out the audit procedures for quality assurance and the new government agency, and recommended that new funding councils should be given the responsibility of ensuring the quality of teaching and learning in higher education (DES 1991). In 1992, the Further and Higher Education Act brought about the redesignation of polytechnics as universities and the abolition of the CNAA and the Higher Education Inspectorate. The Act also led to the establishment of higher education funding councils in England, Scotland and Wales, which were required by statute to monitor the quality of the programmes that they funded and to ensure value for money. Each funding council set up a Quality Assurance division which, from 1992–3 onwards began, on a subject-by-subject basis, an assessment of funded programmes. Also, in 1992, the Higher Education Quality Council was established (HEQC). This was a UK-wide body owned and funded by all HE colleges and universities. Its principal tasks were to undertake a quality audit of each HE institution over a five-year cycle and to promote quality enhancement.

In 1993, the Conservative government in Britain published a further White Paper on higher education, *Realising Our Potential,* which stated that all universities in Britain were to have the quality of their education provision 'assured', thanks to the introduction of rigorous systems of monitoring, inspection and assessment. The White Paper also called for 'a key cultural change' that would 'enforce accountability' to the taxpayer (DES 1993: 5). In the early 1990s, HEFCE required university departments to submit bids or claims that their teaching standards were excellent, satisfactory or unsatisfactory. Teams of senior academics were then sent into universities to assess and grade the departments. Any provision graded as unsatisfactory was allowed twelve months for rectification of the problems, then funding would be withdrawn. The audit of subjects was first called Teaching Quality Assessment and later Subject Review.

A movement from quality control to quality assurance and enhancement is noticeable in the evolution of formal arrangements. Whereas control implies inspection at the end of the production line, assurance involves auditing mechanisms and systems for quality management embedded in every stage of the production process. The aim is to interrogate the regulatory mechanisms through which quality is assured and enhanced. The Quality Assurance Agency (QAA) ostensibly focuses on organisations' own systems of quality assurance and their own aims and objectives.

In 1997, the National Committee of Inquiry into Higher Education, chaired by Lord Dearing, recommended a number of interventions relating to standards and quality. These have contributed to the terms of reference for the QAA, which was set up in 1997 to co-ordinate the review and report on the performance of higher education institutions. The QAA is contractually linked to the government-controlled funding councils rather than universities. Following the publication of the Dearing Report a second agency was also established: the Institute of Teaching and Learning. This aimed to provide professional development and accreditation of teachers in higher education.

The 2003 White Paper (DfES) suggested further amendments. These included the establishment of Centres of Excellence to reward good teaching and promote best practice; the creation of new national professional standards for teaching; and a new national body to develop and promote good teaching – the Teaching Quality Academy.

The QAA oversees the quality assurance of teaching and learning, as well as developing benchmarks, qualifications frameworks and programme specifications; subject assessors and institutional reviewers are recruited from the academic community. In England, Subject Review was first introduced in 1993. From April 1995 to December 2001 six aspects of teaching and learning were audited: learning resources; curriculum development and organisation; teaching, learning and assessment; quality management and enhancement; student progress and achievement; and student support. There was an Aspect Group meeting for each area, in which assessors interrogated staff. Often, staff were required to produce further documentary evidence, at short notice, as a consequence of concerns raised by assessors in Aspect Group meetings. Each aspect was scored out of four and the highest score for an institution was 24. There were three sources of data: observation of teaching sessions, interviews with students, staff and employers and scrutiny of documentation. A base room had to provided by every organisation to contain volumes of information about courses, quality assurance procedures, organisational policies, samples of student work, minutes of meetings, information to students, etc. The assessment of teaching and learning has moved from Subject Review (known as TQA – Teaching Quality Assessment – until 1995) to Institutional Audit. Subject Review involved the inspection and scoring of 42 disciplinary areas, awarding a score for six areas of provision on a four-point scale with a total score of 24. The emphasis in the new system of Institutional Audit is on the institution, rather than on subject areas. For some, Subject Review was viewed as a valuable opportunity for organisational development and reflection, while others experienced it as a highly corrosive form of performance and regulation (Morley 2003).

The assessment of both research and teaching and learning has been a highly controversial enterprise in Britain. Pressure from the CVCP/Universities UK, elite organisations and letters to the media coagulated to produce the need for political action in relation to Subject Review. On 22 March 2001, the Secretary of State for Education announced in Parliament that changes were to be made in the way quality is audited. He announced that the number of review visits would be cut by 40 per cent. University departments that had received good scores, i.e. 21 or over in Subject Review, were to be exempt from external review in the next round. In August 2001, John Randall, the Director of the QAA, resigned in protest because he was unable to accept that the methodology adopted in the new policy was sufficiently rigorous.

In the transition period from Subject Review to Institutional Audit, two consultation documents were published. The first was *Quality Assurance* in Education (QAA 2001). The second, *Information on Quality and Standards of Teaching and Learning: Proposals for consultation* (HEFCE 2002a), was published by a committee, chaired by Professor Ron Cooke, to investigate what public information on quality and standards could be made available to the public. More controversy raged in early 2002 as Margaret Hodge, the Higher Education Minister at the time, refused to endorse new proposals for Institutional Audit, as she disagreed with a 'lighter touch' and felt that new proposals were 'insufficiently rigorous to ensure public accountability' (Baty 2002). The issue of what constitutes appropriate measures of rigour remains highly contested in the policy domain of quality.

In Britain, quality assurance procedures themselves have been subjected to continuous improvement over the years. Over the past twenty years, higher education has been regulated by at least three forms of external scrutiny. First, in the late 1980s, the Committee of Vice Chancellors and Principals (CVCP) established an Academic Audit Unit. This later became incorporated into the Higher Education Quality Council. Second, the Further and Higher Education Act of 1992 dissolved the Council for Academic Awards (CNAA) and invested funding councils with statutory responsibility for quality assessment of the educational provision that they funded. A third strand relates to the arrangements for accreditation of programmes of study leading to professional 'licence to practice'. In this case, higher education has continued to operate in partnership with professional bodies such as the Royal College of Nursing, the British Psychological Society, the Royal Institute of Chartered Surveyors, etc. Stakeholders are proliferating as higher education is now operating in wider professional and international markets.

Britain's claim to fame is that it currently has the most audited higher education system in the world (Cowen 1996). I have given papers and keynote addresses around the world on this subject and am usually met with disbelief over the complexity, extent and cost of quality assurance arrangements in Britain.

Thoroughly modern methods?

Quality assurance is located within the systematic discourse of modernism. There are elements of positivism, with reviewers claiming to be able to unearth a 'truth' about the complexities of organisational life, simply by consulting the 'right' documents and asking the 'right' people. The readings become 'truths', encoded in league tables and reified for several years. This is in direct opposition to postmodern and feminist research paradigms that suggest multiple readings, situated interpretations and discontinuities. Strathern (2000b: 313) notes that 'There is an assumption that a university is first and foremost an organisation whose performance can be observed'. The crisis of representation and the plurality of texts are not considered in quality assessment. There are limited opportunities for interpretative pluralism.

Quality assurance has acquired a discursive orthodoxy in higher education, with material and symbolic consequences. While quality assurance is concerned with fitness for purpose, a question arises as to whether quality technologies themselves are fit for academic purposes. Complex organisations are granularised, i.e. reduced to a myriad of parts and reconstituted to represent a 'pure' whole, containing certain knowledge about processes and practices (Guile 2001). Universal pragmatics has begun to emerge which justify the development and application of quality assurance practices to the academy. However, there are questions about what constitutes evidence and how this is constructed and evaluated. The methodology, particularly for auditing the quality of teaching and learning, has also been criticised for being too 'soft' and open to distortion. In a major form of recuperation of power after their 2001 Subject Review, economists at Warwick University wrote that:

> The method is not scientific. We supplied the hypothesis, the evidence and the witnesses. We chose the students and employers, the samples of student work, and the internal documentation to be seen by the panel.
>
> (*Guardian* 2001)

Scores in Subject Review were not absolute, since they related to how providers met their own aims and objectives. There are questions about who constitutes the self in self-assessment. Whatever the ideological hue to methodological criticisms, there are widespread beliefs that the methodology of quality assessment is characterised by *ad hocery*, instability and unreliability.

4 Reining in

Accountability, autonomy and the audit culture

Accountancy and accountability are frequently elided in quality assurance. The audit culture combines powerful moral reasoning with the methodology of financial accounting. Accountability in higher education appears to be a democratising discourse. However, it is value-laden in so far as it privileges certain types of knowledge, pedagogies, outcomes and management processes over others. Accountability is a commonsense term that over-simplifies power relations. The moral implications overshadow political agendas. Ball *et al.* (1997) offer two broad categories of accountability – market and political. They outline a trend towards the privileging of market accountability over political accountability. Vidovich and Slee (2001: 432) distinguish four main types of accountability: professional accountability to peers; democratic accountability to the community; managerial accountability to governments; and market accountability to customers. In the context of quality assurance accountability appears to be reduced to a type of penance for former autonomy.

A potent binary is the accountability/autonomy two-step. Barnetson and Cutright (2000: 289) argue that accountability is that which is exchanged for autonomy in an authority relationship. Studies on academic identity have emphasised disciplinary culture and academic autonomy (Becher 1989; Becher and Trowler 2001; Clark 1987; Fulton 1996). Mourning the loss of academic autonomy raises questions about transitions to more relational *modus operandi*. Autonomy can be understood as lack of vulnerability to others, a kind of solipsism or lack of sociality or imperviousness that ignores community and proximity. Autonomy is also associated with the elite who can protect their boundaries. For example,

Trowler (1998) questions whether the culture of academic autonomy extended to the former polytechnics, where there was local educational authority control and, indeed, a different client group.

Autonomy is unproblematically positioned as a neutral or potentially benign concept. Berdahl (1990) argued that academic freedom and institutional autonomy are not the same thing. Informants in Kogan and Hanney's study (2000) believed that the power of institutions has grown at the expense of individual academic freedom. Strathern (2000b: 309) cautions that 'visibility as a conduit for knowledge is elided with visibility as an instrument of control'. She asks what visibility also conceals. The relationship between the known/visible and the unknown/invisible is rarely examined.

Audit is increasingly seen as a substitute for professional ethics and an infringement of professional autonomy. In terms of higher education, Strathern (2000a: 2) observes that specific procedures have 'come to carry the cultural stamp of accountability, notably assessments that are likened to audit'. Giddens (1984: 30) suggests that being 'accountable for one's activities is both to explicate reasons for them and to supply normative grounds whereby they might be justified'. Quality assurance is strengthened by the repudiations it implies. It is hard to contest. Power (1994) argues that critics of accountability and audit always appear to be defending elitism, secrecy and privilege.

Delanty (2001) argues that accountability is part of a move towards market values. If everything is driven by profit motives, there needs to be an external form of regulation, as one can no longer rely on intrinsic commitment, professional values and motivation. Henkel (2000) discovered that her informants associated accountability with increasing student numbers and a declining resource base. Staff in some of the pre-1992 universities believed that it was an attempt to impose centralised systems similar to those in the post-1992 universities. Underlying this was an assumption that a mass system could not rely on intrinsic motivation. Professionalism was being replaced by external monitoring systems. Readings (1996) locates current constructions of accountability within the logic of contemporary capitalism. This logic is riddled with norms and power operates by techniques of normalisation. As such, accountability is a major form of power.

Regulating research

In Britain, research is currently audited via the Research Assessment Exercise (RAE). This is a mechanism for distributing funding. It operates by the bestowal and withdrawal of resources. The University Grants Committee first established this system in 1985 and the first RAE was undertaken in 1986, followed by similar exercises in 1992, 1996 and 2001. The aim is the norm-referenced assessment of research against a standard ranging from international excellence to below national excellence.

The system relies on peer review. A committee or panel of researchers from the disciplinary field evaluates the intellectual quality of a piece of research. The assessment process employed is a largely subjective judgement of worth (Whittington 1997). Assessors read the work submitted and grade it on its quality. A common complaint is that the appointment of assessors and decisions about the composition of the panels are not transparent or democratic (Lee and Harley 1998). Furthermore, the emphasis on disciplinary classifications can place interdisciplinary writers at a disadvantage. The concept of excellence is also seen as unstable, or a 'floating signifier' (Lawson 1998). Another aspect of the RAE is the quantification of the number and proportion of 'research active' staff. The results determine the allocation of funding to individual institutions. Hence, there is considerable managerial pressure exerted to make staff more research active as this has tangible financial rewards. The individual writer/researcher has been reconceptualised as an economic agent or unit of resource. Scholarship has been reduced to income generation and entrepreneurship.

The RAE is both a mechanism for the allocation of funding and a system of kitemarking. It functions to rationalise the stratification of research resources and the stratification of universities (Henkel 1999). It also aims to maximise and reward research output. Research productivity has become synonymous with quality. The 2003 White Paper (DfES) refers to 'Best' Universities and 'Teaching' Universities. It also claims that the RAE has undoubtedly led to an overall increase in research quality over the last fifteen years.

Arguments rage about whether quality or quantity has increased. There seems little point in increasing quality or quantity when the budget allocation process is a zero sum game. In 1992 the highest rated department received 4 times the amount of funds paid to the lowest funded department for the same volume of research activity, while in 1996 it received 4.05 times more (Talib and Steele 2000). In 1996, 192 institutions submitted 2,896 individual assessments to the 69 subject area panels (Bainbridge 1998). In 2001, 2,598 submissions were received from 173 institutions, listing the work of 50,000 researchers (HEFCE 2002b). Fifty-five per cent of researchers are currently in 5 or 5* rated departments, compared to 31 per cent in 1996 and 23 per cent in 1992. Eighty per cent of the researchers whose work was assessed were in submissions receiving one of the three top grades (4, 5, and 5*). Formula funding models serve policy objectives. Furthermore, policy objectives are affecting the construction of the labour force and employment regimes. The McNay Report on the 1996 RAE (1997) showed that institutions were focusing on whom they should recruit for research, and how they should reward and retain existing staff. His staff survey results had 12 per cent of the recent appointees, i.e. those less than one year in post, say that the RAE was the most dominant factor in their appointment.

The Research Assessment Exercise has recently been reviewed by a panel chaired by Sir Gareth Roberts (Roberts 2003). Seven key themes emerged from the review:

- the importance of expert peer review
- the need for a clear link between assessment outcomes and funding
- the need for greater transparency, especially in panel selection
- the need to consider carefully the trade-off between comparability of grades and the flexibility for assessors to develop methods appropriate to their subject
- the need for a continuous rating scale

- the need for properly resourced administration of the RAE
- consistency of practice across panels.

Considerable attention was paid to the need to reduce the administrative burden. However, it appears that this is merely being relocated to higher education institutions.

Recommendations for change include: extending the assessment period to six years, with a light touch mid-point monitoring; institutional-level assessments of research competencies, undertaken two years before the main assessment; separate consideration of the least research-intensive institutions; 20 to 25 units of assessment panels; abolition of the rule that each researcher may only submit up to four items; discipline-specific performance indicators; increased transparency in the appointment of panels. One of the most welcome recommendations from the report was the inclusion of equality of opportunity as a concept and practice. Gender was also included as a consideration in the composition of the panels. The report states that:

> The funding councils should monitor and report upon the gender balance of sub-panel members, sub-panel chairs, panel chairs, moderators and senior moderators.
>
> (Roberts 2003: 17)

Leonard (2001: 17) pointed out how, in the 2001 RAE, fewer than one in four panel members and only one in seven of the panel chairs were women, and that the panels chaired by women were responsible for allocating less than 10 per cent of RAE funding. However, the Roberts Report contains a curious mix of democratising interventions and those designed to increase stratification and differentiation. It naturalises social divisions and focuses on the deficit of the less research-active institutions, rather than the privilege of the institutions with high RAE scores. Despite the proposed changes, the RAE will continue to represent an economy of performance, with considerable symbolic power (Henkel 1999).

Performance indicators: the myth of measurement

The economy of performance is made possible partly by the technology of performance indicators. Performance indicators translate macro policies into micro practices. Accounting systems have been invented to calculate individual academics' and academic units' research and publication productivity and 'effectiveness' in teaching quality. These accounting systems represent an encodement of values and priorities. They also structure and construct desires, aspirations and ambition. While purporting to provide consumers with a basis for selection and funders with evidence of output, performance indicators also provide powerful managerial imperatives. They combine description with prescription and mediate between outcomes and goal-setting. Performance criteria tend to be centrally determined. The task of university managers is to facilitate a culture of commitment to them (Taylor 2001). There has been a marked trend towards internalising audit functions and increasing an organisation's and an individual's capacity for self-inspection. A new disciplinary grid has been imposed (Shore and Wright 1999).

Financial instability tightens the grip of performance indicators. Barnetson and Cutright (2000: 281) note the use of 'financial rewards and punishments to manipulate institutional behaviour'. Performance indicators are often allied to competitive bidding procedures. The evaluative information generated by performance indicators can be linked to funding, as with the Research Assessment Exercise in the UK. Hence, performance indicators actively structure rather than simply measure the academy. Regulation can produce the object that it claims to discover. Barnetson and Cutright (2000: 277) believe that performance indicators are 'conceptual technologies' in so far as they shape what issues we think about and how we think about these issues by embedding normative assumptions into the selection and structure of those indicators. They are omnipresent and are part of new managerialism's dispersed responsibility (Clarke and Newman 1997; Bruneau and Savage 2002).

Performance indicators and taxonomies of effectiveness are often little more than socially constructed floating signifiers (Ball 2000; Morley and

Rassool 1999). For example, priorities shift geographically and historically. Performance indicators capture panics, prejudices and fears at any one particular political and historic moment. The certainty of such taxonomies denies any consideration of alternatives. Kaufmann (1988) argues that there are five elements to which performance indicators can be applied: inputs, processes, products, outputs and outcomes. There is an assumption that so-called 'causal' factors are 'independent, universal and additive; that is, they do not interfere with each other and are uninfluenced by contexts' (Hamilton 1998: 15). While they appear neutral, e.g. student completion rates, they are policy instruments to advance a political agenda. Performance monitoring is driven by external requirements for accountability and also by internal mechanisms linked to institutional performance. Forms of action are normatively and communicatively achieved via staff development and employment conditions, e.g. appraisal, or the use of short-term contracts.

Performance indicators are part of the risk society. They are potent signs offering some sort of order and certainty in complex organisations. They are also linked to the principles of consumer entitlement. Nowadays, the public are deemed to be at as much risk from a failing public service organisation as they are from faulty engines on aircraft. Middleton (2000: 542) argues that performance indicators 'are firmly established as a tool of strategic state-managerial control and the assumption is that if universities fail to provide public assurance of quality and standards, more stringent government intervention can be expected'.

An argument in favour of performance indicators is that they summarise complicated processes in at-a-glance information for consumers. Laurillard (1980: 187) observes that performance indicators 'reduce a complexity of subjective judgements to a single objective measure'. Strathern (2000b: 314) argues that there is a translation across domains – from service to assessment – and the language of the indicators eventually takes over the language of the services. Polster and Newsom (1998) suggest that performance indicators make it possible to replace substantive judgements with formulaic and algorithmic representations. However, feedback on performance is frequently incomplete, partial, situated and open to a range of interpretations. Normative obligations are interpreted, conveyed and justified via language, and particular terms have been identified to signify complex processes, e.g. transparency. The observers and the observed have to learn how to exchange information within prescribed signifiers in order to justify claims to authenticity. It is questionable what opportunities there are for interpretative and evaluative differences.

Quality is defined in ever-changing configurations. Academics and managers suffer from policy fatigue. As soon as they learn to decode one set of performance indicators, the indicators change. The transience produces a sense of erasure and negation. Achievement is easily undone. Herein lies a paradox: quality assurance is meant to regulate chaos but it ends up producing it. Turbulence is a relay of power encapsulated in economic theories promoted by the Austrian School, for example. Hayek is one of the theorists who celebrates the benefits of permanent disequilibrium (Middleton 2000). This pattern was noted by Shore and Wright, who report a comment from a HEFCE official at a 1993 Conference of the Society for Research in Higher Education:

> A HEFCE official admitted that performance indicators should only have a shelf life of about two years because 'after that people get wise to them'. The undeclared policy, therefore, is to keep systems volatile, slippery and opaque.
>
> (Shore and Wright 1999: 569)

A further strategy of domination in the assessment of teaching quality is the introduction of arbitrary performance indicators internally and externally, at any point of the proceedings. This is justified in terms of the open-endedness of continuous improvement. This can resonate with academic training, making academics feel as if they will never achieve closure. Turbulence is manufactured in order to avoid any suggestion of stagnation. Higher education is attempting to emulate the change-driven cultures of many profit-motivated corporations (Birnbaum 2000).

The emphasis is on the ability to adapt to turbulent markets rather than to stabilise, and, as numerous theorists of public service organisations have noted, we have to live with ambiguity, uncertainty and constant change (Hassard and Parker 1993; Reed and Hughes 1991). While organisations invest large sums in uncertainty avoidance, responsiveness to change is itself a performance indicator.

5 The political is personal

The psychic economy of quality

There is a psychic economy involved in quality assurance. Quality assessment, accountability and the auditing of academic work have had a profound impact on reconstructing academic conditions of work and academic identities. The academic *habitus* has been challenged. Academics have to be simultaneously self-managing and manageable workers who are able to make themselves auditable within prescribed taxonomies of effectiveness. There is a new cultural logic governing academic professionalism (Walker 2001). These cultural and political changes demand additional temporal and material investments. They also involve significant emotional labour. Anxieties, aspirations and fears invade people's interior spaces, as every individual working in academia is made aware that their performance, productivity and professional conduct is constantly under scrutiny within non-negotiable frameworks.

Issues of quality and standards take on a particularly emotive tone (Case *et al.* 2000). The academy has long represented the life of the mind. In line with the Cartesian dualism, emotions and embodiment have been largely understated in the quest for abstract knowledge. Traditional myths, symbols and rituals of universities have centred on carefully choreographed ceremonies, control and constraint. The detached, cold and emotionally inept academic has become a professional stereotype. Indeed, in traditional, positivistic academic culture, impersonality was presented as the hallmark of quality and reliability. Emotion was a signifier of bias and unreliable knowledge. In the 'pop' psychology text Goleman (1996) cites academics as exemplars of a professional group with low emotional intelligence. However, recent accounts of life in the academy suggest that strong emotions are surfacing. There have been reports on occupational stress, the long hours culture and the requirement for academics to provide emotional support for an ever-increasing number of diverse students (AUT 1998; Fisher 1994; Malina and Maslin-Prothero 1998; Morley 2003).

Professional identity is essentially socially mediated. There is a strong relationship between public discourse and social and professional identities. There is an element of intersubjectivity in the constitution of identity. Hence, public 'discourses of derision' (Ball 1990: 31) can be internalised and believed at some level. Traditionally, universities have been able to assign individuals with a ready-made identity embedded in notions of social hierarchy. Now professional identities are constantly in flux. It is not enough simply to reproduce the skills and knowledges for which one was originally appointed. There is an imperative to be entrepreneurial, innovative and to add value to one's organisation. This multiskilling creates anxieties about maintaining expertise. Jarvis (2000: 45) observed that no matter how hard academics argue for their independence, they will be forced to respond to the infrastructural social pressures that shape the world as a whole. McWilliam *et al.* (1999: 62) observe that there is the emergence of an instrumental workplace culture that is centred on 'galvanising the economic potential of knowledge'. Academics are being asked to reinvent themselves, their courses, their cultural capital, and their research as marketable commodities.

For some, quality assurance can represent an area of danger in the academy (Wyn *et al.* 2001; Douglas 1966): danger in so far as the purity of disciplinary divisions is being contaminated with bureaucracy, but also danger in the sense of witch-hunts and blame culture. For example, Ramsden (1998) suggests that individuals who resist quality management of their performance should be identified in order to maximise the performance of their organisation. Danger also exists in the form of a threat to professional autonomy, for example the sense of invasion and powerlessness to control one's time, priorities and objectives. Quality assurance is presented as a consensual discourse yet it produces system-induced identity threats. Henkel (2000: 96) found that for her academic informants the audit of teaching and learning quality was 'a dramatic intervention in their working lives, dominating the semester or term in which it occurred, and the whole academic year for those with responsibility for organising it'. Arrangements for quality assessments are making academics and administrators increasingly mutually dependent. Academics and administrators are forced to provide more documentary evidence as proof of their professionalism and competence. There are internal and external audiences, resulting in multiple accountancy pressures and high visibility and vulnerability.

Quality assurance involves making distinctions – classifying, segregating, drawing boundaries – dividing people and organisations into categories simultaneously united and separated by similarity and difference (Bauman 2001a). A resignifying process takes place. Some people are authorised to speak authoritatively because others are silenced. A question remains as to whether the culturally constructed subject can rewrite the script when all resistance is perceived as defensive action. Some do succeed in strategically mobilising neo-liberal discourses for counter-hegemonic challenges, e.g. equity issues (see Luke 1997). For others, a safer strategy is simply to perform (Morley 2003).

Performativity and the power of discourse

Performativity can involve a damaging process of ventriloquism and impersonation as academics and managers attempt to represent themselves in a language that quality assessors will understand and value. For some it implies a lack of ideological control over the task. For others, it is a game (Morley 2003). Producing the right kind of optimistic and promotional self-description in mission statements, vision statements and self-assessment documents incorporates self-subversion and ritualistic recitation and reproduction. Womack (1999) observes that the language of authority works not only by what it says to us, but also by what it induces us to say. The text-producers in quality assurance, according to Cameron (2001), are not just passive recipients of other people's propaganda, but have been induced to create their own. Oswald (2001: 15) reminisces that 'When I was a young lecturer, universities were the one place in the country where you could not bluster your way through life. Hype was useless; content was everything'.

The (hyped) text is complicit in the reproduction of quality norms. The slow subjection of individuals involved in quality assurance takes place via language and the authoritative power of text. Organisations are compelled to repeat the norms of quality assurance in all its documentation. Failure to reinstate the norm in the right way opens up the possibility of sanctions. Hence considerable effort is invested in the preparation of documentation, codes of practice and textual representation.

Academics have to operate without and within the quality discourse (Henkel 2000). Being watched makes them watchful. Continuous improvement is linked to what Pels (2000: 136) describes as a liberal constitution of the self. This is 'a schizoid modern self that is both the object of improvement and the subject that does the improving'. Academics have to move between the objectified and the objectifier. Womack (1999: 5) argues that being the assessed and the assessor at the same time means that 'we assert our self but also act out the role of the other; we speak as the child seeking approval but imitate the booming voice of the father who may bestow or withhold it. In short, our prose keeps stumbling because it is schizophrenic'. Gewirtz *et al.* (1995) name the process of educationalists negotiating two or more sets of values and cultures as 'bilingualism'. Different linguistic codes are invoked in appropriate contexts to represent different values and priorities. However, performance and ventriloquism can create cognitive dissonance and alienation.

Giddens (1990: 6) recognises that modern institutions 'hold out the possibility of emancipation but at the same time create mechanisms of suppression, rather than actualisation, of self'. The proliferation of critical literature on quality from across the globe suggests that some spaces have been opened up for a certain type of democratic contestation. However, the protests remain largely at the level of text, e.g. angry letters and articles in the public press and memoranda to the QAA. Direct action to resist the quality industry carries too many financial penalties. Current funding arrangements operate to suppress critical engagement. Cameron (2001: 103) points out how the system of representing one's organisation in glowing terms in self-assessment documents, for example, is a convenient mechanism for the government, which underfunds Britain's public institutions. She argues that institutions can be relied on 'to produce, apparently of their own free will and in their own words, an endless flow of discourse in which their services are represented as excellent and constantly improving; where problems are trivial (and always already in the process of being solved), and where catastrophic failures are non-existent'. Academics are being forced to create their own propaganda to promote the practices that many of them criticise.

Performativity is linked to discourse. Fraser (1997) suggests that the conception of discourse can illuminate how the cultural hegemony of dominant groups in society is secured and contested. Hegemony is the discursive face of power. Fraser also argues (p. 160) that discourses are 'historically specific, socially situated, signifying practices'. She sees them as 'communicative frames in which speakers interact by exchanging speech acts'. Discourse frames practice and the way in which practice is discussed and conceptualised. Dominelli and Hoogvelt (1996: 84) suggest that it is through discourse and practice that 'the individual and the group gradually become drawn into a new world of lived experience that gradually detaches them from their own critical consciousness, ideology or value commitments'. The quality discourse is engulfing professional consciousness and dominating organisational priorities. Butler (2000: 108) claims that 'If the power of discourse to produce that which it names is linked with the question of performativity, then the performative is one domain in which power acts as discourse'.

Lyotard (1984) argued that universities are structured around bounded discourses including disciplines, faculties and professorial authority. New managerialism has reinforced performance discourses. Staff have performance reviews, individuals and departments are required to have performance targets, there is talk of introducing performance-related pay in universities, as in the schools sector (Shore and Selwyn 1998). Lyotard (cited in Dhillon and Standish, 2000) points out that one of the dangers of performativity is that any new moves that are made, anything that looks like becoming critical, can be encompassed and assimilated. As with any powerful metanarrative asserting 'truths', other 'truths' are silenced and excluded from the quality discourse.

The imperative to perform and conform is antithetical to the expansionist culture of the 1960s' higher education system in Britain. Between 1963 and 1973 there was an increase in full-time tenured academic staff from 16,881 to 26,429. Dominelli and Hoogvelt (1996: 72) argue that the expansion 'provided a home for intellectuals critical of society looking for alternative visions'. They identify two categories of intellectuals:

> the professional bureaucratic/technocratic intellectuals or 'hegemonic' organic intellectuals who serviced the welfare state and endorsed the Establishment in its activities; and the critical thinkers or 'counter-hegemonic' organic intellectuals who organized around welfare issues and demanded changes in welfare state structures, including the delivery of personal social services, as well as more radical changes in the allocation of power and distribution of resources in society.
> (Dominelli and Hoogvelt 1996: 72)

Quality assurance has demanded that all academics display characteristics of the 'hegemonic' rather than counter-hegemonic intellectuals. Any analysis of power and power relations has to be suspended while performing technocracy. When the ratio of inner beliefs to public presentation changes dramatically, this can produce feelings of being duplicitous and inauthentic.

Performativity is not fun, as in playfulness. It is not a way to find expression, but to repress it. Ball (2000) sees performativity as a technology, a culture and a mode of regulation through which power operates. Performances act as measures of productivity or displays of quality. In the context of quality assurance, performativity is the reverse of carnival. The subversive value of representation is questionable. It is the period of dis-licence in which every utterance must be carefully censored. Referring to teaching quality assessment, Shore and Selwyn observe:

> we find ourselves in educational spaces which have become theatres: where classrooms become 'stages', teachers and students 'actors'

(performing to a script imposed upon them by government), and where inspectors, journalists and 'market forces' act as audience and critics.
(Shore and Selwyn 1998: 162)

Goffman's theory of dramaturgical compliance (see, for example Goffman 1972) suggests that the theatricality involved in performance can serve to protect and distance actors from the corrosive effects of alien bureaucratic requirements. They employ role distance in order to reintroduce a sense of personal autonomy (Case *et al.* 2000). In his study of quality procedures in New Zealand's higher education sector, Barrow (1999: 34) notes how staff aim to present themselves in a positive light in ways appropriate to the particular role and setting. A question arises as to whether there is a fundamental injustice involved in requiring professionals to represent themselves in terms and roles that are alien. However, this can also be seen as academia's coming of age.

The stress of split focusing

The different accounting systems mean that academics, like many other professional groups, have become split subjects, simultaneously interpellated in different ways and caught in damaging oscillations. There are questions about the oppositional and complementary relationship of teaching and research (Robertson and Bond 2001). Time spent on developing teaching quality is time away from research productivity and *vice versa*. Yet quality research is also seen to enhance teaching quality by ensuring that lectures are informed by latest studies and research findings However, conditions of labour and production are often at odds with each other. McInnis (2000) reports that the policy imperative to improve quality teaching at the same time as demanding more research output is placing academics under 'enormous pressure' (p. 150). Academics have to spend more time supporting students with a wide range of abilities, more time on pastoral care and engage to a far greater extent with new technologies for teaching. Fuller describes how research and teaching used to complement each other:

teaching curbed the esoteric tendencies of research, while research disrupted the routinising tendencies of teaching.... However, this delicate balance between the two functions is in danger of being lost. On the one hand, teaching is being reduced to the dispensation of credentials; on the other, research is being privatised as intellectual property: the one driven by the employment market, the other by the futures market.

(Fuller 1999: 587)

Whatever the activity, the market is the driving force. The university is sometimes referred to as a 'bundle' institution (Delanty 2001; Habermas 1992) in so far as it combines a range of functions including the research process, general education, the training of future professionals and the formation of public opinion. The professional self has been fragmented into 'researcher', 'administrator', 'teacher' and more recently 'entrepreneur'. According to Habermas (1992) this reflects the complex position of the university, which he sees as being located between social and cultural structures on one hand, and the system of money and power on the other. In relation to quality assessment, academics have to negotiate a range of roles in order to perform in the various categories that mark out the inspection of their work.

The issue of split focusing is vexing many academics. Talking of academics, Oshagbemi (1996: 390) notes that 'Hardly any other group of workers performs such a disparate array of functions'. Many of the demands that appear to be exceeding the capacity of academic labour relate to quality assurance procedures (Morley 2003). A discourse of loss is often evident in studies of higher education today. The coming of quality represents a type of death of the previous academic *modus operandi*. The nostalgia can sometimes constellate around a normatively construed former age. This is accompanied by a type of grief, mourning or sense of dispossession in the transformation process. Some losses are ungrievable, e.g. loss of precariousness, the hidden curriculum and underperformance, while others are grievable, e.g. loss of control over use of time and loss of intellectual complexity in the over-simplification of market values.

6 In the long term

While the over-elaborate Subject Review finished in Britain at the end of 2001, the ethos of beratement and surveillance has continued in a new structural guise. This is proliferating internationally with policy borrowing moving across networks and traffic flows. Quality assurance has contributed to the reconfiguration of academic *habitus*. New discursive constellations, employment regimes and multi-skilling have produced disruption, cognitive dissonance and dislocation. For some this is embraced as progress and innovation, for others it is experienced in terms of enhanced workload, occupational stress and domination. For some, quality assurance provides a fixed point of reference in a changing higher education policy context. It represents a creed, a catechism or a *modus operandi*. For many, the methodology of QA is perceived as taking the academy backwards in terms of sophistication of analysis (Morley 2003). Discourses in education policy documents, concerning the knowledge society of the twenty-first century, are often to be found accompanied by quality assurance discourses based on a positivistic epistemology from the nineteenth century.

Loss is becoming constitutive of current academic identity. In quality assurance, loss of autonomy, for example, is constructed as a consequence of fault, and is therefore ungrievable. Current loss of autonomy is becoming equated with future loss of human resources. In the Kantian tradition, the university has traditionally been a site of critique. The quality movement in higher education has compromised and muted the possibilities for critical engagement with the technologies used to assure quality. It demands compliance and performativity and the endless reproduction of norms. Delanty (2001: 73) talks about the need for 'a zone of engagement between power, knowledge, politics and culture'. The university could occupy that zone. However, there are fears that intellectually able and critical staff will exit to escape unacceptable regulation and surveillance. Organisations and individuals are berated by a constantly shifting ideal. Quality assurance is perceived as an instrument of containment, in opposition to critique and intellectual creativity

Paradoxically, the culture of excellence is producing mediocrity. The compliance culture and command economy in higher education threatens to produce self-policing, ventriloquising apparatchiks, as opportunities for cultural agency are reduced. Wolf (2001: 17) asserts that 'under-funding, uniformity and death by intrusive inspection - that is the road to ruin. The consequences are foreseeable: ill-paid and demoralised functionaries will take the place of independent and innovative scholars'. Cameron (2003) also explores the issue of low morale and calls upon the Chancellor of the Exchequer to reflect on who will be left to teach the expanded student base by 2010.

The controversial Higher Education Bill scraped through its first reading in January 2004. This has confirmed a system of new funding mechanisms, with the introduction of variable top-up fees from 2006. Higher education has become more visibly a market with the potential for further organisational and social stratification. Once students and their families become liable for up to £3,000 a year in fees alone, their consumer status will be strengthened. Hence, the prediction is for more emphasis on quality assurance and value for money. The academy can look forward to yet more regulation and surveillance.

Quality assurance is a socially constructed domain of power. As a discourse, it wields the power to form and regulate through the imposition of its own terms. Workers in the academy have had to incorporate and internalise it for their professional and organisational survival. Hence, it has become difficult to contest. Quality assurance demands a self- and organisation beratement that demoralises and disempowers. Quality assurance discursively carries the threat and trace of the other within it. Resistance cannot be easily declared because it implies espousal of the other side of quality, that is – privilege, elitism, mystification of decision-making, unreliability and shoddiness. Opposition is not easily communicative, since to oppose quality is to become its opposite. Excessive volumes of work involved in preparation compound disempowerment. The processes inflict a type of social, psychic and organisational violence and trauma.

Constant change, unpredictability, instability and disequilibrium are part of social and organisational life (Cutright 2001). For some, quality assessment has transformative potential and is perceived as part of the democratising process in which students and other stakeholders have a more formalised structural position in relation to organisational development and the maintenance of professional standards. For others, quality assessment is unstable, unreliable and undesirable. In this analysis, some aspects of higher education are perceived as non-narratable and cannot be tied to the conceit of transparency. Furthermore, quality assessment produces normative aspirations in the midst of considerable diversity. Some members of the academy occupy multiple subject positions in relation to quality, seeing it almost in postmodern terms. For them, it is a regime of truth with both positive and negative potential (Morley 2003).

The narrative grammar of quality is characterised by articulations of ambivalence. Some members of the academy occupy a liminal position – operating within and outside quality assurance. For some, quality assurance has provided new paradigms for thinking about academic work and new career opportunities. For others, it is about suspicion, mistrust and the management of processes, rather than standards, with considerable wastage and frustration involved. As a new disciplinary technology it has exacerbated old or introduced new power relations. Quality assessment imposes a fiction of coherence and unity on an otherwise fragmented set of academic functions and services. The imposition of interpretation and scoring on multiple academic realities has created potential both for accolades and for misrecognition and inequalities. For many, it has been a form of symbolic violence.

References

Association of University Teachers (AUT) (1998) *Pressure Points – a survey into the causes and consequences of occupational stress in UK academic and related staff*. London: AUT.

Bacchi, C. (2000) 'Policy as discourse: what does it mean? Where does it get us?' *Discourse: studies in the cultural politics of education* 21(1): 45–57.

Baimbridge, M. (1998) 'Institutional research performance 1992–1996: a tale of two sectors.' *Journal of Further and Higher Education* 22: 69–78.

Ball, S.J., (1990) *Politics and Policy Making in Education: Explorations in policy sociology*. London: Routledge.

—— (1998) 'Performativity and fragmentation'. In J. Carter (ed.), 'Postmodern schooling'. London: Routledge.

—— (2000) 'Performativities and fabrications in the education economy: towards the performative society?' *The Australian Educational Researcher* 27(2): 1–23.

—— (2003) 'The teacher's soul and the terrors of performativity'. *Journal of Education Policy* 18(2): 215–28.

Ball, S.J., Vincent, C. and Radnor, H. (1997) 'Into confusion: LEAs, accountability and democracy'. *Journal of Education Policy* 12(3): 147–64.

Barnetson, B. and Cutright, M. (2000) 'Performance Indicators as conceptual technologies'. *Higher Education* 40(3): 277–92.

Barnett, R. (2000) *Realizing the University*. Buckingham: SRHE/Open University.

Barrow, M. (1999) 'Quality management systems and dramaturgical compliance'. *Quality in Higher Education* 5(1): 27–36.

Baty, P. (2002) 'Fury as Hodge calls the shots'. *Times Higher Education Supplement*. 22 February.

Baudrillard, J. (1998) *The Consumer Society*. London: Sage.

Bauman, Z. (2001a) *The Individualized Society*. Malden, MA: Polity Press.

—— (2001b) *Community: Seeking safety in an insecure world*. Cambridge: Polity Press.

Becher, T. (1989) *Academic Tribes and Territories: Intellectual enquiry and the cultures of disciplines*. Milton Keynes: Society for Research into Higher Education/Open University Press.

Becher, T. and Trowler, P. (2001) *Academic Tribes and Territories: Intellectual enquiry and the cultures of disciplines* (2nd edition). Buckingham: Open University.

Beck, U. (1997) *The Reinvention of Politics: Rethinking modernity in the global social order*. Cambridge: Polity.

Beilharz, P. (ed.) (2001) *The Bauman Reader*. Oxford: Blackwell.

Berdahl, R. (1990) *British Universities and the State*. New York: Arno.

Berry, C. (1999) 'University League Tables: artefacts and inconsistencies in individual rankings'. *Higher Education Review* 31(2): 3–10.

Billing, D. and Thomas, H.G. (1998) 'Quality management and organisational structure in higher education'. *Journal of Higher Education Policy and Management* 20(2): 139–59.

Birnbaum, R. (2000) *Management Fads in Higher Education*. San Francisco: Jossey Bass.

Bologna Declaration (1999) Online. Available HTTP: http://www.bologna-berlin2003.de/pdf/bologna_declaration.pdf (accessed 14 July 2004)

Bowden, R. (2000) 'Fantasy higher education: university and college league tables'. *Quality in Higher Education* 6(1): 41–59.

Brigham, S. (1993) 'TQM: ten lessons we can learn from industry'. *Change* 25: 42–8.

Bruneau, W. and Savage, D. (2002) *Counting Out the Scholars: How performance indicators undermine universities and colleges*. Toronto: CAUT/James Lorimer and Co.

Butler, J.P. (1997) *The Psychic Life of Power: Theories in subjection*. Stanford, CA: Stanford University Press.

Butler, J. (2000) *Contingency, Hegemony, Universality: Contemporary dialogues on the left / Judith Butler, Ernesto Laclau and Slavoj Žižek*. London, Verso.

Cameron, D. (2001) 'Mission impenetrable'. *Critical Quarterly* 43(2): 99–103.

——(2003) 'Doing exactly what it says on the tin: some thoughts on the future of higher education'. *Changing English* 10(2): 133–41.

Cameron, K. and Ettington, D. (1988) 'Conceptual foundations of organisational culture'. In J.C. Smart (ed.) *Handbook of Theory and Research*. New York: Agathon.

Case, P., Case, S. and Catling, S. (2000) 'Please show you're working: a critical assessment of the impact of OFSTED inspection on primary teachers'. *British Journal of Sociology of Education* 21(4): 605–21.

Clark, B. (1987) *The Academic Life*. Princeton: Carnegie.

Clarke, J. and Newman, J. (1997) *The Managerial State*. London: Sage.

Coaldrake, P. (2000) 'Rethinking academic and university work'. *Higher Education Management* 12(3): 7–30.

References

Coate, K., Court, S., Gillon, E., Morley, L. and Williams, G. (2000) *Academic and Academic Related Staff Involvement in the Local, Regional and National Economy.* London: Association of University Teachers/Institute of Education, University of London.

Cooper, D. and Subotsky, G. (2001) *The Skewed Revolution: Trends in South African higher education 1988–1998.* Bellville: University of the Western Cape, Education Policy Unit.

Cowen, R. (1996) 'Performativity, post-modernity and the university'. *Comparative Education* 32(2): 245–58.

Cutright, M. (ed.) (2001) *Chaos Theory and Higher Education: Leadership, Planning, and policy.* New York: P. Lang.

Dearing, R. (1997) *Higher Education in the Learning Society* (Dearing Report) London: National Committee of Inquiry into Higher Education.

Dearlove, J. (1997) 'The academic labour process: from collegiality and professionalism to managerialism and proletarianisation?' *Higher Education Review* 30: 56–75.

Deem, R. (2001) 'Globalisation, new managerialism, academic capitalism and entrepreneurialism in universities: is the local dimension still important?' *Comparative Education* 37(1): 7–20.

Delanty, G. (2001) *Challenging Knowledge: The university in the knowledge society.* Buckingham: Open University Press.

Deming, W. (1986) *Out of the Crisis: Quality, productivity and competitive position.* Cambridge, Cambridge University Press.

DES (Department of Education and Science) (1991) *Higher Education: A new framework.* London: HMSO.

DfES (Department for Education and Skills) (2003) *The Future of Higher Education.* London: DfES.

—— (1993) *Realising Our Potential: A strategy for science, engineering and technology,* Cm 2250. London: HMSO.

Dhillon, P. and Standish, P. (eds) (2000) *Lyotard: Just education.* London: Routledge.

Dill, D. (2001) 'The regulation of public research universities: changes in academic competition and implications for university autonomy and accountability'. *Higher Education Policy* 14(1): 21–35.

Dominelli, L. and Hoogvelt, A. (1996) 'Globalization, contract government and the Taylorization of intellectual labour in academia'. *Studies in Political Economy* 49: 71–100.

Douglas, M. (1966) *Purity and Danger: An analysis of concepts of pollution and taboo.* London, Routledge and Kegan Paul.

Dreyfus, H. and Rabinow, P. (1982) *Michel Foucault: Beyond structuralism and hermeneutics.* Brighton, Harvester Press.

Etzkowitz, H. and Leydesdorff, L. (ed.) (1997) *Universities in the Global Economy: A triple helix of university, industry, government relations.* London: Cassell.

Fisher, S. (1994) *Stress in Academic Life: The mental assembly line.* Milton Keynes: Open University Press/Society for Research in Higher Education.

Fraser, N. (1997) *Justice Interruptus: Critical reflections on the 'postsocialist' condition.* New York: London, Routledge.

Fuller, S. (1999) 'Making the university fit for critical intellectuals: recovering from the ravages of the postmodern condition'. *British Educational Research Journal* 25(25): 583–95.

Fulton, O. (1996) 'The academic profession in England on the eve of structural reform'. In P. Altbach (ed.), *The International Academic Profession.* Mento Park: Carnegie Foundation.

Gale, T. and Kitto, S. (2003) 'Sailing into the wind: new disciplines in Australian higher education'. *British Journal of Sociology of Education* 24(4): 501–14.

Gewirtz, S., Ball, S.J. and Bowe, R. (1995) *Equity, Markets and Choice.* Buckingham: Open University.

Giddens, A. (1984) *The Constitution of Society: Outline of the theory of structuration.* Cambridge: Polity.

—— (1990) *The Consequences of Modernity.* Cambridge, Polity.

Goffman, E. (1972) *Interaction Ritual: Essays on face-to-face behaviour.* Harmondsworth: Penguin.

Goleman, D. (1996) *Emotional Intelligence: Why it can matter more than IQ.* London: Bloomsbury.

Guardian (2001) 'Trial By Ordeal'. 30 January: 12.

Guile, D. (2001) MA Seminar at the University of London Institute of Education, 13 March.

Habermas, J. (1992) 'The Idea of the University – learning processes'. *The New Conservatism: Cultural criticism and the historians' debate.* Cambridge: Polity Press.

Hamilton, D. (1998) 'The idols of the market place'. In R.W. Slee, G. Weiner and S. Tomlinson (eds), *School Effectiveness for Whom? Challenges to the school effectiveness and school improvement movements.* London: Falmer Press: 13–20.

Handy, C. (1993) *Understanding Organisations.* Harmondsworth: Penguin.

Harari, O. (1993) 'Ten reasons why TQM doesn't work'. *Management Review* 82(1): 33–8.

Hart, W.A. (1997) 'The Qualitymongers'. *The Journal of the Philosophy of Education Society of Great Britain* 31(2): 295–308.

References

Hassard, J. and Parker, M. (1993) *Postmodernism and Organisations.* London, Sage.
HEFCE (Higher Education Funding Council of England) (1992) *Quality Assessment.* Circular 10/92. Bristol: HEFCE.
—— (1993) *The Review of the Academic Year* (Flowers Report). London: Higher Education Funding Council for England (HEFCE).
—— (2002a) *Information on Quality and Standards in Higher Education: Final report of the Task Group.* Bristol: HEFCE.
—— (2002b) *2001 Research Assessment Exercise: The outcome.* Bristol: HEFCE.
Henkel, M. (1999) 'The modernisation of research evaluation: the case of the UK'. *Higher Education* 38: 105–22.
—— (2000) *Academic Identities and Policy Changes in Higher Education.* London: JKP.
HEQC (Higher Education Quality Council) (1997) *The Graduate Standards Programme: Final report.* London: HEQC.
Hodson, P.J. and Thomas, H.G. 'Towards an enterprise culture: will the Quality Assurance Agency help or hinder?' *Higher Educational Review* 3, 2(1): 24–33.
Howie, G. (2002) 'A reflection of quality: instrumental reason, quality audits and the knowledge economy'. *Critical Quarterly* 44(4).
Jarvis, P. (2000) 'The changing university: meeting a need and needing to change'. *Higher Education Quarterly* 54(1): 43–67.
Jenkins, P. (1999) *Synthetic Panics: The symbolic politics of designer drugs.* New York: New York University Press.
Kaufman, R. (1988) 'Preparing useful performance indicators'. *Training and Development Journal* September: 80–3.
Keller, G. (1992) 'Increasing quality on campus: what should colleges do about the TQM mania?' *Change* May–June: 48–51.
Kogan, M. and Hanney, S. (2000) *Reforming Higher Education.* London: Jessica Kingsley.
Laurillard, D. (1980) 'Validity of Indicators of Performance'. In D. Billing (ed.), *Indicators of Performance.* Guildford: SRHE.
Lawson, A. (1998) 'Culture and utility: phrases in dispute'. In D. Jary and M. Parker (eds), *The New Higher Education: Issues and directions for the post-Dearing university.* Stoke-on-Trent: Staffordshire University Press: 273–7.
Lee, F. and Harley, S. (1998) 'Economics divided: the limitations of peer review'. In D. Jary and M. Parker (eds) *The New Higher Education: Issues and directions for the post-Dearing university.* Stoke-on-Trent: Staffordshire University Press: 185–206.
Leonard, D. (2001) *A Woman's Guide to Doctoral Studies.* Buckingham: Open University Press.

Levin, B. (1998) 'An epidemic of education policy: what can we learn from each other?' *Comparative Education* 34(2): 131–42.

Lingard, B. (2000) 'It is and it isn't: vernacular globalization, educational policy, and restructuring'. In N. Burbules and C. Torres (eds), *Globalization and Education: Critical perspectives*. London: Routledge: 79–108.

Lucas, L., and Webster, F. (1998) 'Maintaining standards in higher education? A case study'. In D. Jary and M. Parker (eds), *The New Higher Education*. Stoke-on-Trent: Staffordshire University Press: 105–13.

Luke, C. (1997) 'Quality assurance and women in higher education'. *Higher Education* 33: 433–51.

Lyotard, J. (1984) *The Postmodern Condition*. Manchester: Manchester University Press.

McInnis, C. (2000) 'Changing academic work roles: the everyday realities challenging quality in teaching'. *Quality in Higher Education* 6(2): 143–52.

McNay, I. (1997) *The Impact of the 1992 RAE on Institutional and Individual Behaviour in English Higher Education*. Bristol: HEFCE.

McRobbie, A. (1994) *Post-Modernism and Popular Culture*. London: Routledge.

McWilliam, E., Hatcher, C. and Meadmore, D. (1999) 'Developing professional identities: remaking the academic for corporate times.' *Pedagogy, Culture and Society* 7(1): 55–72.

Malina, D. and Maslin-Prothero, S. (eds) (1998) *Surviving the Academy: Feminist perspectives*. London: Falmer.

Manicas, P. (1998) 'Higher education at risk'. *Futures* 30(7): 651–6.

Margolis, E., (ed.) (2001) *The Hidden Curriculum in Higher Education*. New York and London: Routledge.

Middleton, C. (2000) 'Models of state and market in the "modernization" of higher education'. *British Journal of Sociology of Education* 21(4): 537–53.

Morley, L. (2003) *Quality and Power in Higher Education*. Buckingham: Open University Press.

—— (2004, in press) 'Sounds, silences and contradictions: gender equity in Commonwealth higher education – Clare Burton Memorial Lecture 2003'. *Australian Feminist Studies*.

Morley, L. and Rassool, N. (1999) *School Effectiveness: Fracturing the discourse*. London: Falmer.

NIACE (1993) *Learning to Succeed*. London: Heinemann.

Nisbet, R. (1971) *The Degradation of Academic Dogma: The university in America, 1945–70*. London: Heinemann.

OECD (1995) *Performance standards in education: in search of quality*. Paris: OECD.

Oshagbemi, T. (1996) 'Job satisfaction of UK academics'. *Educational Management and Administration* 24: 389–400.
Oswald, A. (2001) 'Kick teaching inspectors out of universities'. *The Sunday Times*. 1 April: 15.
Ozga, J. and Walker, L. (1999) 'In the company of men'. In S. Whitehead and R. Moodley (eds), *Transforming Managers*. London: UCL Press: 107–19.
Pattern, J. (1993) 'Only quality can save universities'. *The Times*. 6 December.
Pels, P. (2000) 'The trickster's dilemma: ethics and the technologies of the anthropological self'. In M. Strathern (ed.), *Audit Cultures: Anthropological studies in accountability, ethics and the academy*. London, Routledge: 135–72.
Polster, C. and Newson, J. (1998) 'Don't count your blessings: the social accomplishments of performance indicators'. In J. Currie and J. Newson (eds), *Universities and Globalization: Critical perspectives*. London: Sage: 173–91.
Polster, C. (2000) 'The future of the liberal university in the era of the global knowledge grab'. *Higher Education* 39: 19–41.
Power, M. (1994) *The Audit Explosion*. London: Demos.
—— (1997) *The Audit Society*. Oxford: Oxford University Press.
QAA (2001) *Quality assurance in UK higher education: Proposals for consultation*. Gloucester: Quality Assurance Agency.
Ramsden, P. (1998) 'Out of the wilderness'. *The Australian*. 29 April: 39–41.
Readings, B. (1996) *The University in Ruins*. Cambridge, MA and London: Harvard University Press.
Reed, M. and Hughes, M. (eds) (1991) *Rethinking Organisations*. London: Sage.
Roberts, G.G. (2003) *Review of Research Assessment: Report by Sir Gareth Roberts to the UK funding bodies: issued for consultation May 2003*. Online. HTTP: <http://www.ra-review.ac.uk/reports/roberts.asp> accessed 14 July 2004.
Robertson, J. and Bond, C.H. (2001) 'Experiences of the relation between teaching and research: what do academics value?' *Higher Education Research and Development* 20(1): 5–19.
Sennett, R. (1998) *The Corrosion of Character: The personal consequences of work in the new capitalism*. New York: Norton.
Shore, C. and Selwyn, T. (1998) The marketisation of higher education: management, discourse and the politics of performance'. In D. Jary and M. Parker (eds), *The New Higher Education*. Stoke-on-Trent: Staffordshire University Press: 153–71.
Shore, C. and Wright, S. (1999) 'Audit culture and anthropology: neo liberalism in British higher education'. *Journal of the Royal Anthropological Institute*: 557–75.
Silver, H. (1993) *External Examiners: Changing roles*. London: CNAA.

Sommer, J. (1995) *The Academy in Crisis: The political economy of higher education.* New Brunswick: Transaction Publishers.
Strathern, M. (1997) '"Improving ratings": audit in the British University system'. *European Review* 5(3): 305–21.
—— (ed.) (2000a) *Audit Cultures: Anthropological studies in accountability, ethics and the academy.* London: Routledge.
—— (2000b) 'The tyranny of transparency'. *British Educational Research Journal* 26(3): 309–21.
Talib, A. and Steele, A. (2000) 'The research assessment exercise: strategies and trade-offs'. *Higher Education Quarterly* 54(1): 68–87.
Taylor, J. (2001) 'The impact of performance indicators on the work of university academics: evidence from Australian universities'. *Higher Education Quarterly* 55(1).
Tomlin, R. (1998) 'Research league tables: is there a better way?' *Higher Education Quarterly* 52: 204–20.
Trow, M. (1994) 'Managerialism and the academic profession'. *Higher Education Policy* 7(2): 11–18.
Trowler, P. (1998) *Academics Responding to Change: New higher education frameworks and academic cultures.* Buckingham: Society for Research into Higher Education/Open University Press.
UNESCO (1998) *Towards an Agenda for Higher Education: Challenges and tasks for the 21st century viewed in the light of the regional conference.* Paris: UNESCO.
Vidovich, L. and Slee, R. (2001) 'Bringing universities to account? Exploring some global and local policy tensions'. *Journal of Education Policy* 16(5): 431–53.
Walker, M. (ed.) (2001) *Reconstructing Professionalism in University Teaching.* Buckingham: Open University Press.
Whittington, G. (1997) 'The 1996 Research Assessment Exercise'. *British Accounting Review* 29: 181–97.
Wolf, M. (2001) 'Mediocrity flourishes when an inspector calls'. *Financial Times.* 16 April: 17.
Womack, P. (1999) 'Ac-cen-tchuate the positive'. *CCUE NEWS (Council for College & University English)* 10(Winter): 3–5.
World Bank (1994) *Higher Education: The lessons of experience.* Washington, DC: World Bank.
Wyn, J., Acker, S. and Richards, E. (2000) 'Making a difference: women in management in Australian and Canadian faculties of education'. *Gender and Education* 12 (4): 435–47.